CUVIER'S ANIMALS

867 Illustrations from the Classic Nineteenth-Century Work

GEORGES, BARON CUVIER

Selected and Arranged by

CAROL BELANGER GRAFTON

DOVER PUBLICATIONS, INC.

Mineola, New York

Bibliographical Note

Cuvier's Animals: 867 Illustrations from the Classic Nineteenth-Century Work is a new work, first published by Dover Publications, Inc., in 1996.

DOVER *Pictorial Archive* SERIES

Library of Congress Cataloging-in-Publication Data

Cuvier, Georges, baron, 1769–1832.
    Cuvier's animals : 867 illustrations from the classic nineteenth-century work /
Georges, Baron Cuvier ; selected and arranged by Carol Belanger Grafton.
        p.   cm. — (Dover pictorial archive series)
    Includes index.
    ISBN 0-486-29102-2 (pbk.)
    1. Zoology—Pictorial works.   2. Zoological illustration—Pictorial works.
I. Grafton, Carol Belanger.   II. Title.   III. Series.
QL46.C88   1996
591'.022'2—dc20   96-14919
                                                                                CIP

Manufactured in the United States of America
Dover Publications, Inc., 31 East 2nd Street, Mineola, N.Y. 11501

PUBLISHER'S NOTE

GEORGES, BARON CUVIER (1769–1832) was one of the major
figures in the development of the modern study of natural
history. Initially devoting himself to comparative anatomy,
Cuvier branched out into paleontology, evolving a theory of
Catastrophism to explain what seemed to be the sudden
extinction of species. A prolific author, his major work was *Le
Règne animal distribué d'après son organisation* (1817), in which he
divided animals into four classifications: vertebrate, mollusk,
articulate and radiate. Although this system did not endure, it
marked an important change in approaches to animal
classification.

Le Règne animal was published in many editions and languages,
with various sets of illustrations. Those reproduced here were
selected from an English edition of 16 volumes, *The Animal
Kingdom*, published by Geo. B. Whittaker (later Whittaker &
Co.), London, 1827–35. When possible, captions identify subjects
by their current common names. In some cases, current
scientific names are used. Names within brackets are those
provided in the Whittaker edition, and do not reflect modern
usage.

CONTENTS

1: Capuchin monkey.   2: Chimpanzee.   3: Siamang monkey.   4: Pinche monkey.

5: [Ouanderou].   6: Gibbon.   7: Orangutan.   8: [Maimon].   9: Ruffled lemur.

10: Loris. 10a: Galago. 11: Chinese bonnet monkey. 12: Douroucouli.
13: Cacajo. 14: Howler monkey.

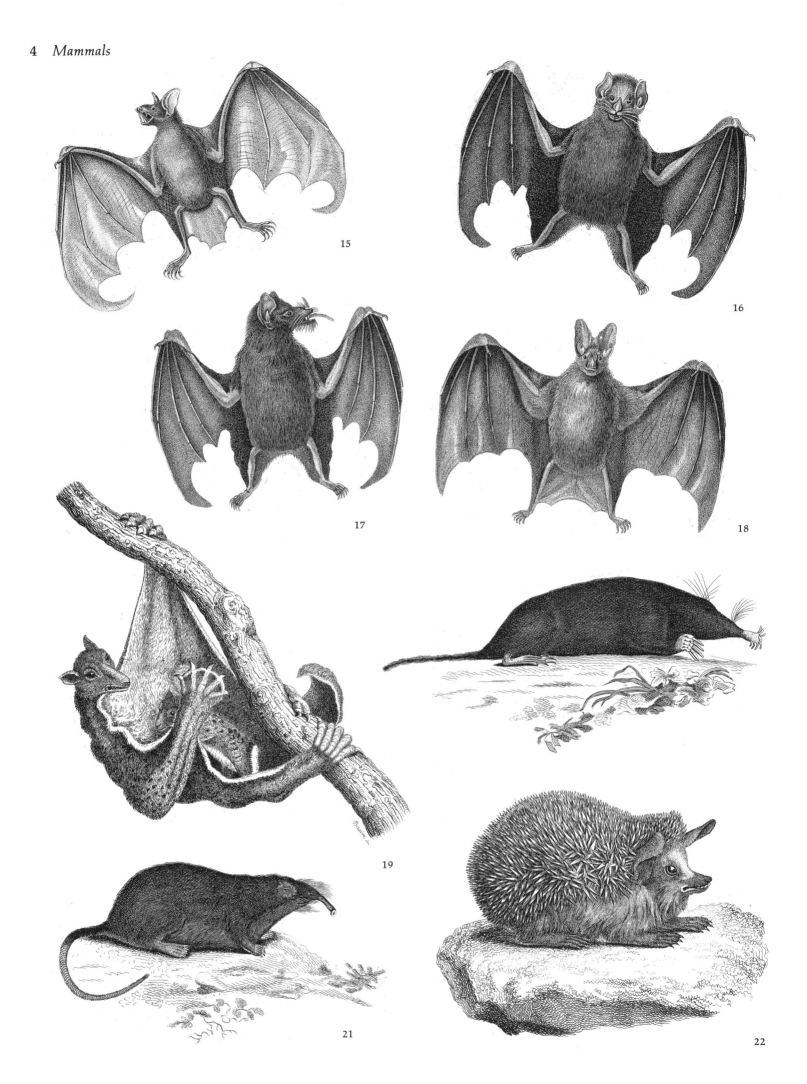

15–18: Bats.   19: Colugo.   20: Star-nosed mole.   21: Pyrenean desman.   22: Long-eared desert hedgehog.

23: Malayan sun bear.   24: Polar bear.   25: Tayra.   26: Masked glutton.

27: Striped skunk. 28: Skunk. 29: Glutton. 30: Weasel. 31: Teledu.

32: Bulldog.   33: Sea otter.   34: Canadian river otter.   35: Greyhound.   36: Alpine
spaniel.   37: Dingo.   38: Mastiff.   39, 40: Wild dogs.   41: Dhole.   42: Wolf.

43, 45: Fennecs.   44: Spotted hyena.   46: Civet.

47

48

49

47: Zibet. 48: Genet. 49: Binturong.

50: Suricate.   51: Palm civet.   52: Tiger.

53

54

55

53: White tiger. 54: Lion–tiger crossbreed. 55: Jaguar.

56: Jaguar. 57: Panther (conjectural earlier form). 58: Once.

59: Panther.   60: *Felis chalybeata*.   61, 62: Ocelots.

14 *Mammals*

63, 65: Ocelots. 64: [Cape cat]. 66: Tiger cat. 67: Pampas cat.

68: Chati.   69: Serval.   70: [Cape cat].   71: Jaguarundi.   72: *Felis macrourus.*

73: Lynx.   74: Eira.   75: Wild tortoiseshell cat.   76: Dolphin.

77, 80: Harp seal.   78: Walrus.   79: Harbor seal.

81: North American opossum. 82: [Touan]. 83: Dasyurus. 84: Water opossum.

85: Clam-eating opossum.   86: Phalanger.   87: Dasyurus.   88: Bandicoot.

89: Greater gliding opossum.   90: Dormouse.   91, 92: Kangaroos.

93: Fat dormouse.   94: Koala.   95: Wood rat.

96: Spiny rat.   97: Coypu.   98: Hamster.   99: Chinchilla.

100: Hyrax.   101–103: Marmots.

104–107: Squirrels.

108–111: Squirrels.   112: Aye-aye.

113: Prairie dog.   114: Tapeti.   115: Porcupine.   116: Aperea.   117: Agouti.

118, 120, 121: Three-toed sloths.   119: Patagonian cavy.

122: Hairy armadillo. 123: Aardvark. 124: Giant armadillo. 125: Lesser anteater.

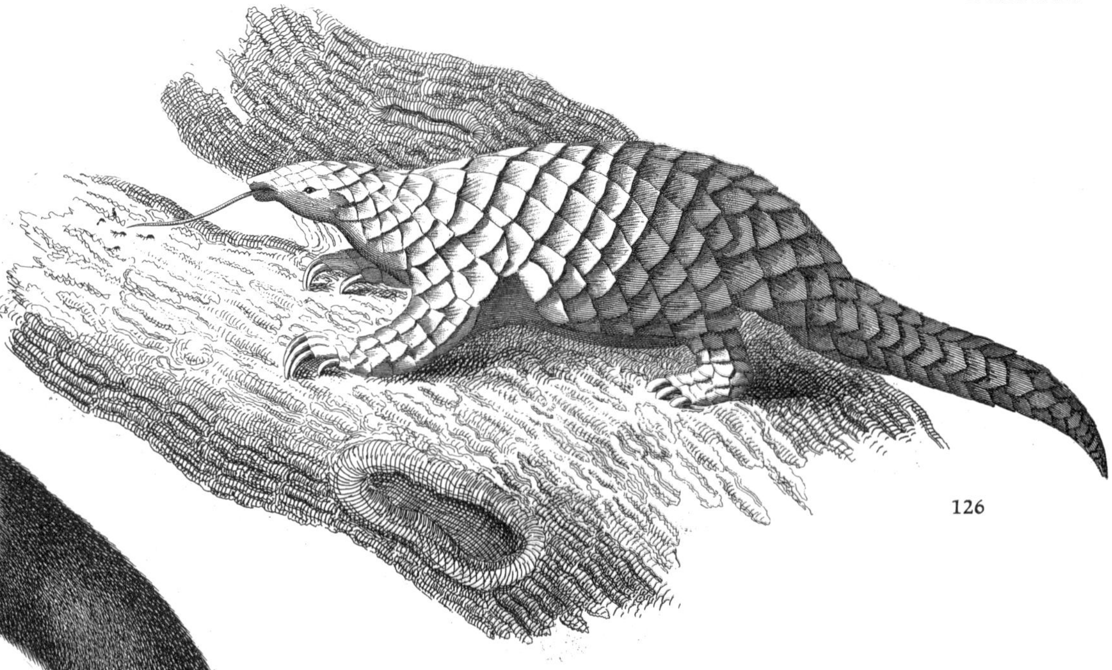

126

127

128

129

126. Pangolin. 127. Lesser Anteater. 128. Platypus. 129. African elephant.

130: White-lipped peccary. 131: Wild boar. 132: African bush pig.
133: Babirusa.

134: Greater Indian rhinoceros.   135: Asiatic tapir.   136: Tapir.   137: Hyrax.

138: Llama.   139: Alpaca.   140: Pygmy musk deer.   141: Musk deer.

142: Wapiti.   143: Alaskan moose.   144: Sambar.

145, 147: Deer.   146: Brocket deer.   148: Philippine sambar.

154: Muntjac.   155: Ootan.   156: Antelope.   157: Ibex.

158: Kob.   159: Bighorn sheep.   160: Caama.   161: Antelope.

162: [*Dicranocerus palmatus*].   163: Eland.   164: Topi.   165: Pronghorn.
166: Cape buffalo (immature).

167: [Pegasse of Angola]. 168: Brindled gnu. 169: [*Dicranocerus palmatus*].
170: Indian water buffalo.

171: Gayal.   172: Wild ox.   173: Bison.

174. Lammergeier.   175, 177. Vultures.   176. Condor.

178: Wedge-tailed eagle.   179: Kite.   180: Harpy eagle.   181: Imperial eagle.

182

183

184

185

186: Supercilious owl.   187: Mississippi kite.   188, 189: Shrikes.

194: *Querula lumachelli.*   195, 196: Thrushes.   197: Grackle.

198: Magpie-lark.   199: Fairywren.   200: Red-bellied pitta.   201: Yellow thorn-
bill.   202: Philedon.

203, 207: Wrens.　204: Nightjar.　205: Fairywren.　206, 208: Swallows.

209

211

210

212

209. Nightjar. 210: Scissor tailed nightjar. 211: Frogmouth. 212: Lark

213: Bunting.   214: Weaver.   215: Finch.   216: Widowbird.   217: Grosbeak.

218

219

220

221

222, 224: Magpies.   223: Roller.   225: Nuthatch.   226: [Long-billed souimanga].

227: Hummingbirds.   228: Mamo (extinct).   229: Giant hummingbird.   230: European bee eater.   231: Bee eater.

232: Bee-eater.   233: Rufous-bellied kookaburra.   234: Blue-winged kookaburra.
235: Tody.   236: Hornbill.

237. Acorn Woodpecker. 238. Woodpecker. 239, 240. Barbets. 241. Koel.

242: Pavonine quetzal.   243: Toucan.   244: Trogon.   245: Parrot.   246: Parakeet.

247

248

249

250

251, 253: Parrots.   252: Cockatoo.   254: Plantain-eater.   255: Cockatoo.

261: Turkey. 262: Horned pheasant. 263: Chestnut-bellied sandgrouse. 264, 265: Pheasants.

266, 267: Grouse   268: Blood pheasant   269: Partridge   270: Quail

271: Grouse.   272: Pigeon.   273: Turtledove.   274: Collared plover. 275: Ostrich.

276: Houbara.   277: Emu (juvenile).   278: Stanley bustard.   279: Crested
cariama

280: Snipe.   281: Gray-winged trumpeter.   282: Agami heron.   283: Heron.

284

285

286

287

284. Boatbill 285. Marabou 286. African openbill 287. Roseate spoonbill

288: Black-faced ibis.   289: Sacred ibis.   290: American avocet.   291: Jacana.

292: Orange-footed scrubfowl.   293: Long-legged plover.   294: Rail.   295: Jacana.

296: Crake.   297: Coot.   298: Rail.   299: Purple gallinule.   300: Gallinule.

301: Greater flamingo. 302: Pratincole. 303: Great crested tern. 304: Black-naped tern.

305: Black-necked swan.   306: Inca tern.   307: Snakebird.   308: Spur-winged goose.

309: Red-billed tropicbird.   310: Northern shoveler.   311: Greylag goose.
312. Goose.   313. Labrador duck (extinct).

314: White-faced whistling-duck.   315: Orinoco goose.   316: Blue-winged teal.
317: Wandering whistling-duck.   318: Common pochard.

319, 320, 322: Tortoises.   321: Leopard tortoise.   323, 325: Turtles.   324: Hinged
tortoise.   326: Soft-shelled turtle.

327: Matamata. 328: Tortoise. 329: Long-necked turtle. 330, 331: Anoles.
332: Turtle.

333. Crocodile. 334, 335, 337. Geckos. 336. Lizard. 338. Caiman.

339: Spiny-tailed lizard.   340: Lizard.   341: Jungle runner.   342: Monitor lizard.

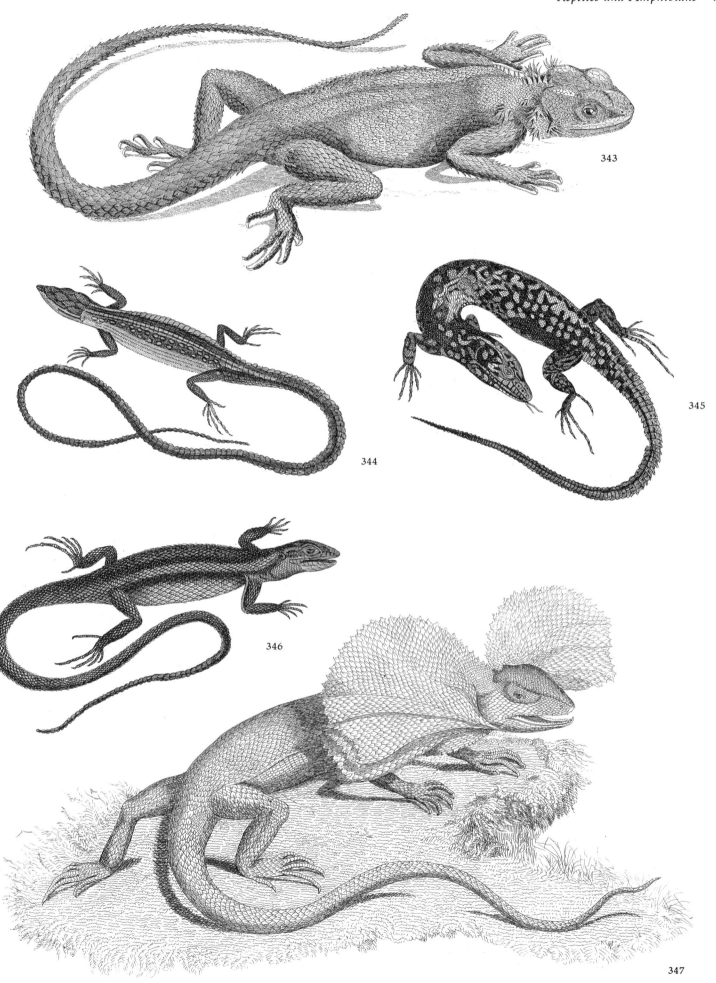

343: Agama.   344, 346: Lizards.   345: Green lizard.   347: Frilled lizard.

348: Anole.   349: Chameleon.   350: Lizard.   351, 352: Horned lizards.

353: Basilisk. 354: Chameleon. 355: Fischer's chameleon.

356: Skink.   357, 358: Snakes.   359: Russell's viper.   360: Viper.

361

362

363

364

361. File snake. 362. Python. 363. Natrix. 364. Boa

365: Snake.   366, 368: Coluber.   367: Amphisbaena.

369

370

371

372: Horned frog.   373: Agua toad.   374: Green toad.   375: Surinam toad.

376, 378. Axolotl.   377. Green frog.   379. Giant salamander   380. Mudpuppy

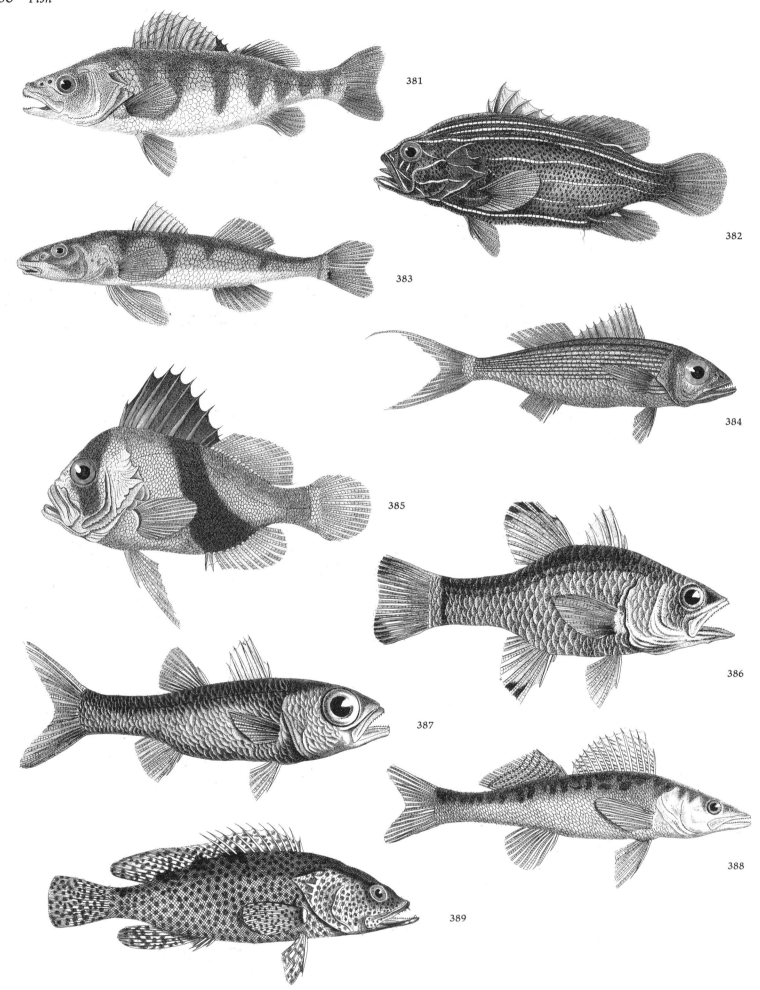

381: Yellow perch. 382: Rockfish. 383: Darter. 384: [*Etelis carbunculus*].
385: [*Diploprion bifasciabon*]. 386, 387: Cardinalfish. 388: Walleye. 389: Nassau
grouper.

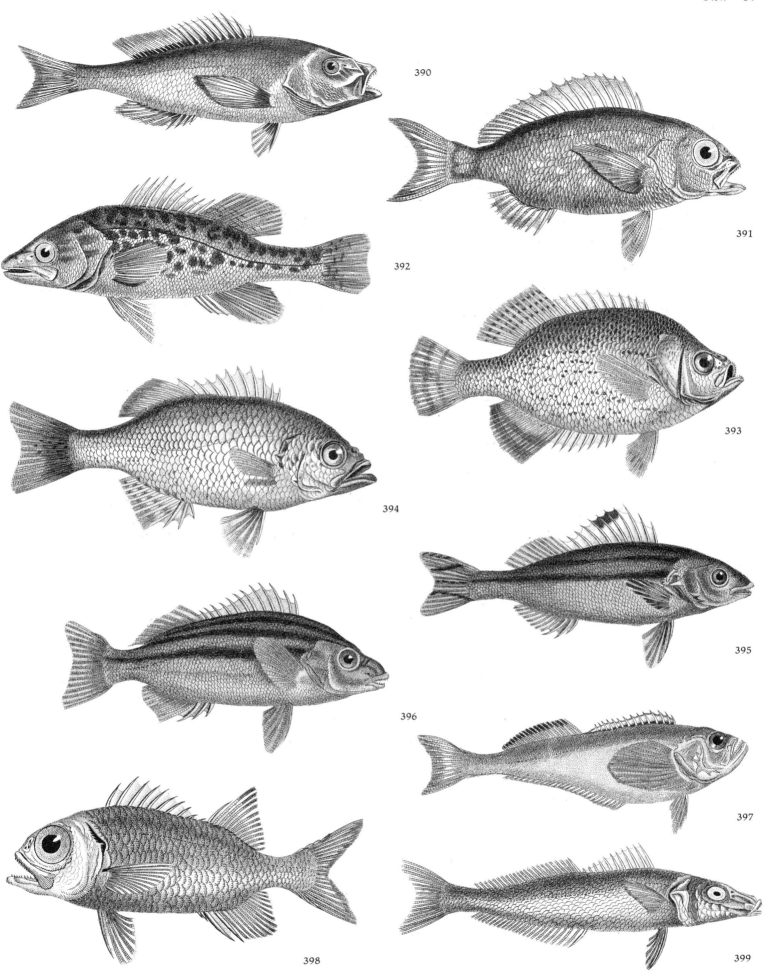

390: [*Mesoprion aya*]. 391: [*Centropristes aurorubens*]. 392: Merou. 393: Crappie.
394: Perch. 395: Rockfish. 396: [*Pelates quadrilineatus*]. 397: [*Trichodon Stelleri*].
398: Blackbar soldierfish. 399: Zander.

400: Berycid. 401: Snakehead. 402: Blenny. 403: [*Polynemus enneadactylus*].
404: John Dory. 405: Stargazer. 406, 409: Barracudas. 407: Scorpionfish.
408: Goatfish.

410: Searobin.   411: Flathead.   412: Gurnard.   413, 418: Sculpins.   414: Flying
Gurnard.   415: Oarfish.   416: Sea poacher.   417: [*Agriopus peruvianus*].   419: [*Taenia-
notus triacanthus*].   420: Sea raven.

421: Spinefoot.   422: Sunfish.   423: Drumfish.   424: Spadefish.   425: Atlantic
mackerel.   426: Angelfish.   427: Wrasse.   428: Gourami.   429: [*Nomeus Peronii*].
430: Sea bass.

431: Black-banded angelfish.   432: [*Dipterodon capensis*].   433: Copper sweeper.
434: French angelfish.   435: [*Psettus rhombeus*].   436: Pompano.   437: Monkfish.
438: Anglerfish.   439: Mullet.

440: Pike.   441: Archerfish.   442: John Dory.   443: Brook trout.   444: Spinefoot.
445: White-throated surgeonfish.   446: Catfish.

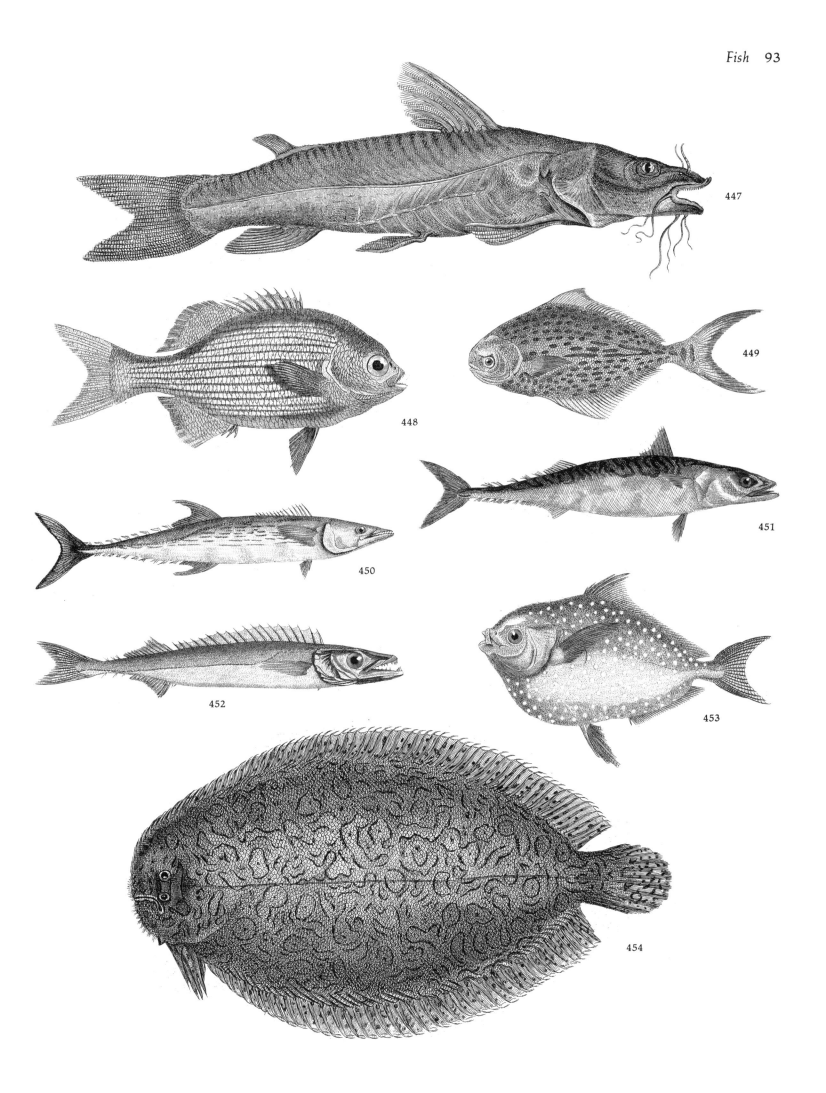

447: Madtom.   448: Cichlid.   449: Butterfish.   450: [*Cybium lineolatum*].   451: Atlantic mackerel.   452: Wahoo.   453: [*Lampris guttatus*].   454: Flounder.

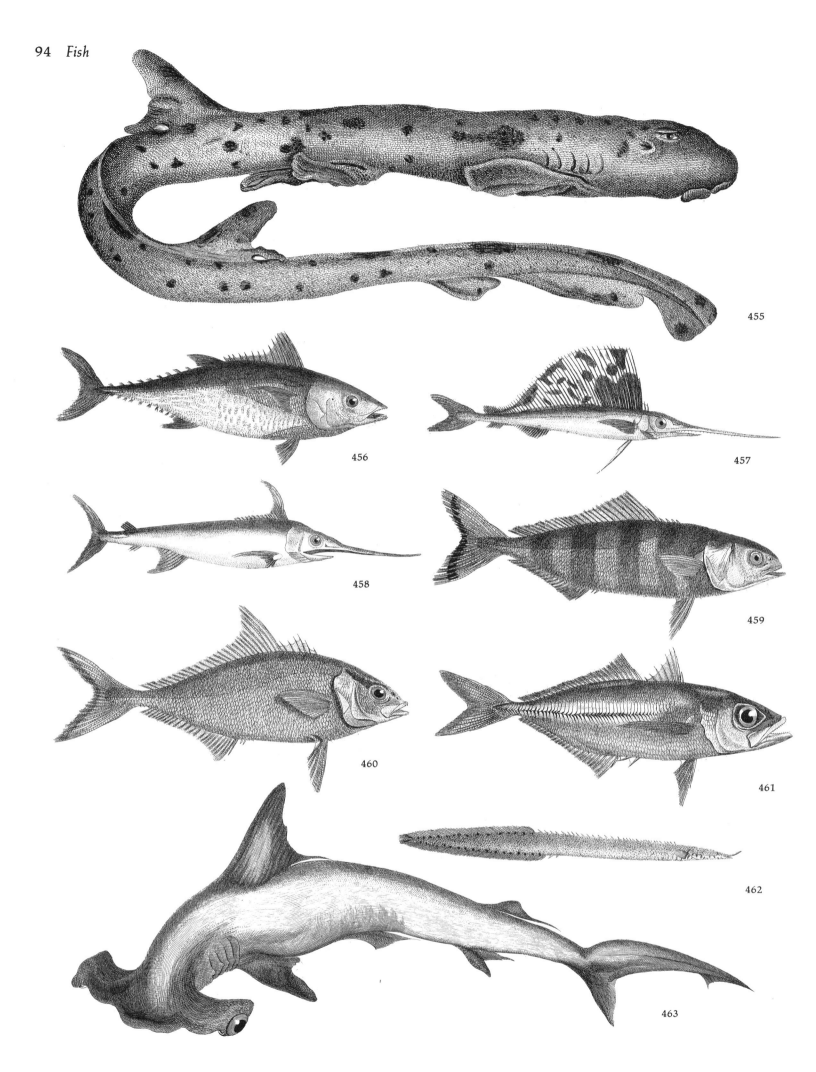

455: Lesser spotted dogfish.   456: Tuna.   457: Sailfish.   458: Swordfish.   459: Pilot fish.   460: Amberjack.   461: [*Caranx boops*].   462: Spiny eel.   463: Hammerhead shark.

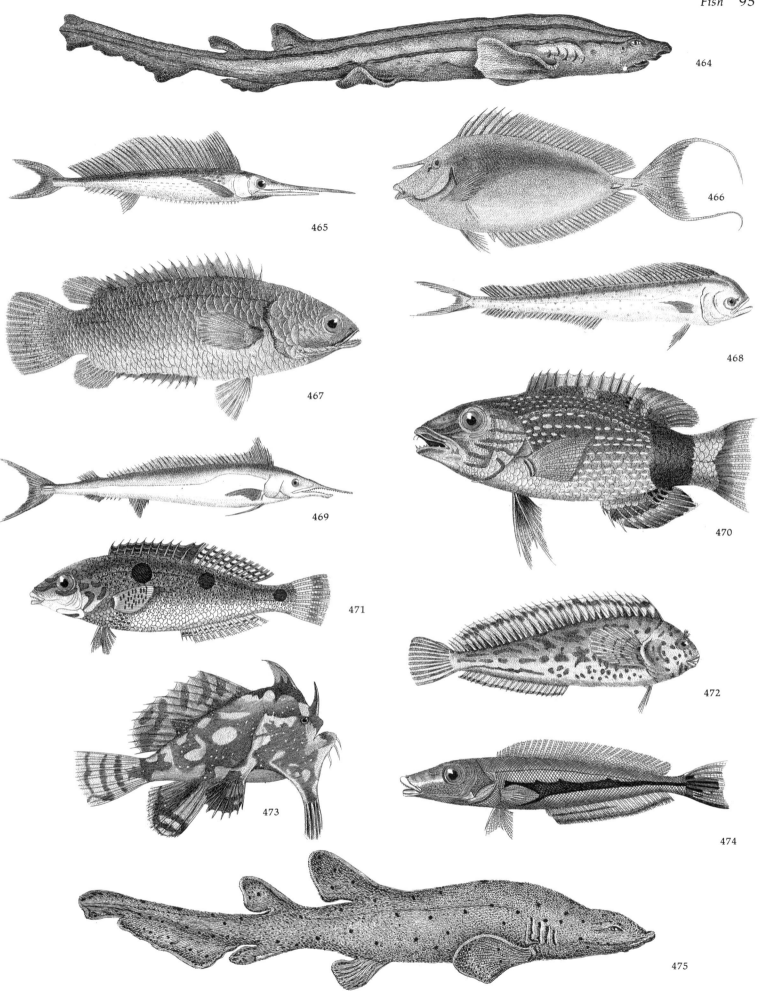

464: Shark. 465: Swordfish (juvenile). 466: Surgeonfish. 467: Gourami.
468: Dolphin. 469: Marlin. 470: Crenilabrus. 471, 474: Wrasses. 472: Boss
blenny. 473: Barb fish. 475: Swell shark.

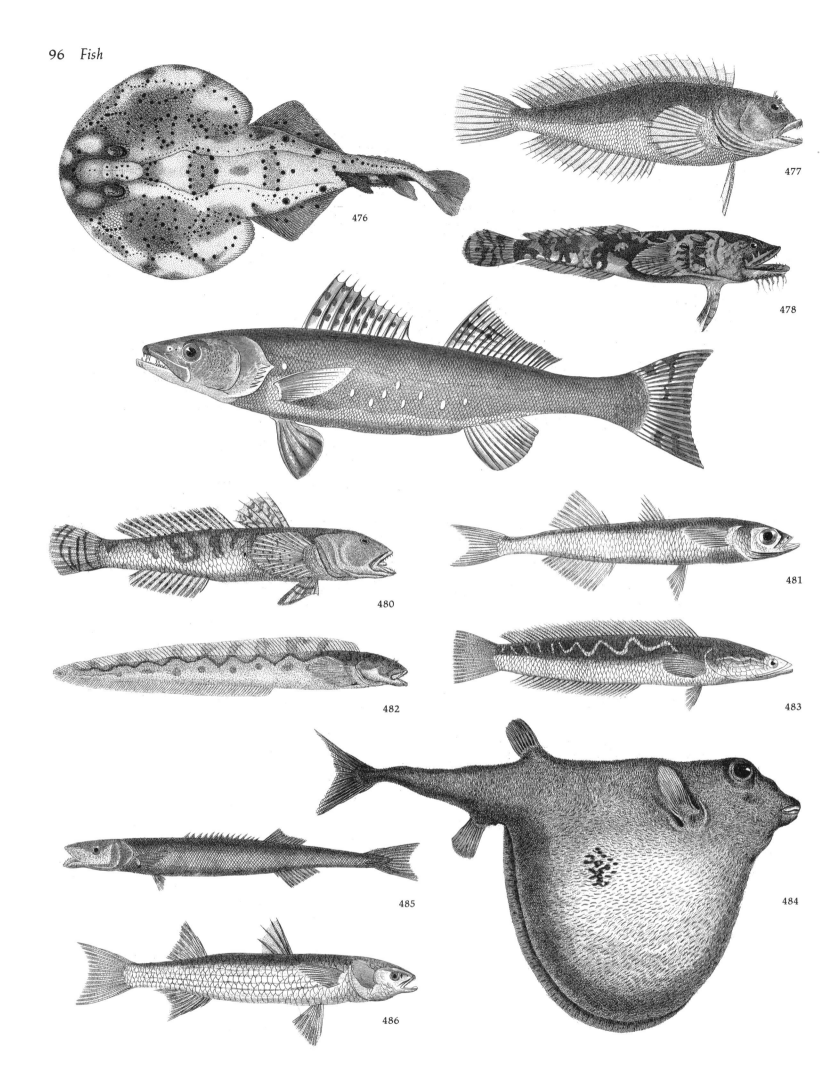

476: Ray.   477: Clinid.   478: Toadfish.   479: Walleye.   480: Goby.   481, 485: Sil-
versides.   482: Cusk-eel.   483: Snakehead.   484: Pursefish.   486: Sablefish.

487: Cuttlefish. 488–490, 493: Slugs. 491, 492: Octopuses. 494: Squid. 495, 496, 500–504: Snails. 497: Chambered nautilus. 498: Freshwater snail. 499: Cerithium.

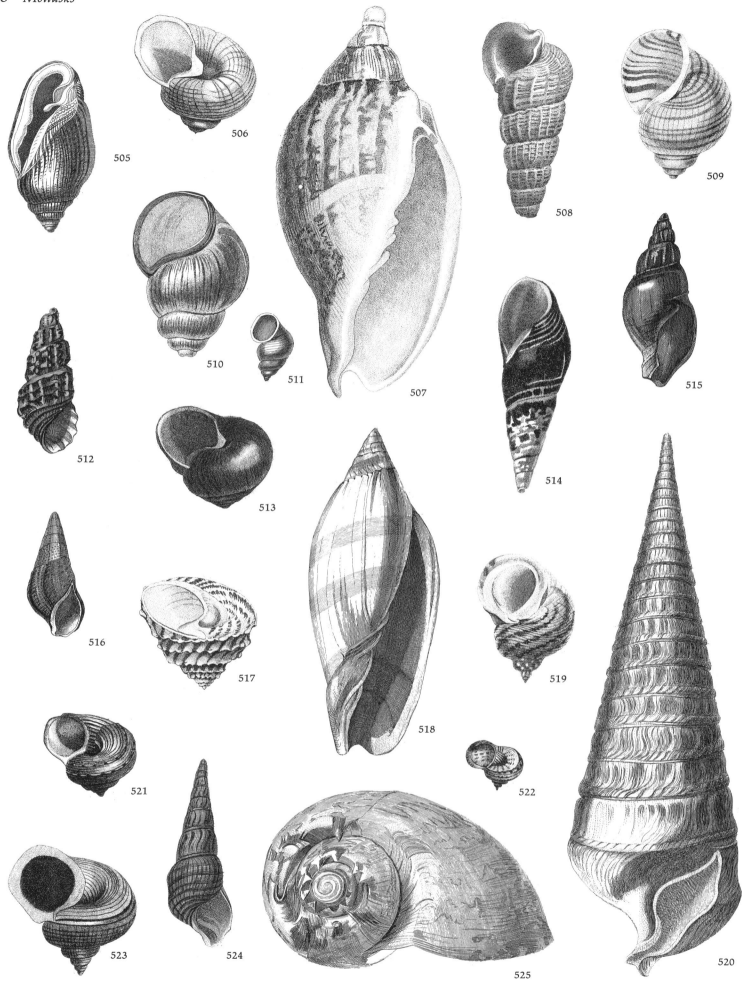

505: Auriculidae.   506, 513, 521–523: Cyclostoma.   507: *Voluta papillosa*.   508, 514, 516, 524: Melania.   509: Freshwater snail.   510: Periwinkle.   511: Unidentified gastropod. 512, 520: Ceriths.   515: [*Nafsa Northiae*].   517: Trochus.   518, 525: Volute.   519: [*Littoria pulchra*].

526: Natica.   527: [*Scarabus impium*].   528: [*Conovolus fasciatus*].   529: Turritella.   530, 541: Turbinella.   531: [*Potamis fragilis*].   532, 543, 546: Volutes.   533: Bulimus.   534: Harp shell.   535: Triton.   536, 548: Miter shells.   537: Dolium.   538: Georgina volute. 539: Conch.   540: Olive shell.   542: Pleurotoma.   544: Pyrula.   545: Pterocera. 547: Auger shell.

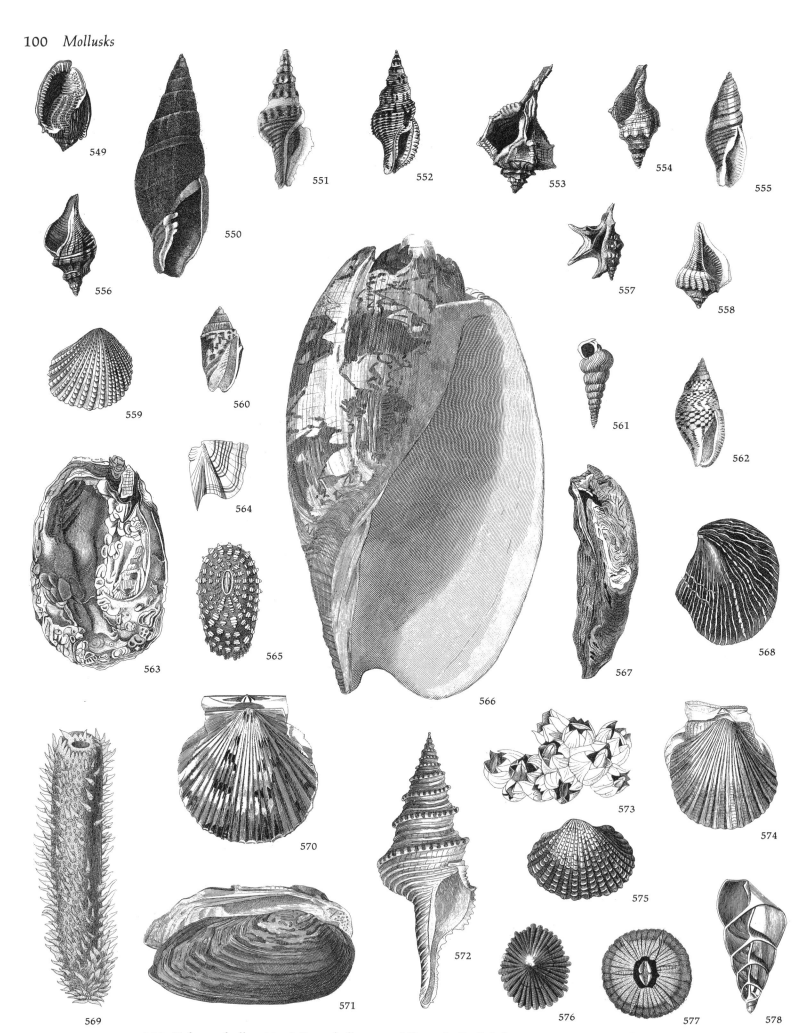

549: Helmet shell. 550: Miter shell. 551: [*Clavatula Griffithii*]. 552, 555: Triton shells.
553: Murex. 554: Tulip shell. 556: Fusus. 557: [*Rostellaria pelspelicani*]. 558: Pyrula.
559: Trigonia. 560: Olive shell. 561: [*Potamis fragilis*]. 562: Dove shell. 563, 567:
Etheria. 564, 575: Ark shells. 565: [*Pyrgoma canellata*]. 566: Volute. 568: [*Crenatula
avicularis*]. 569: Pyrosoma. 570, 574: Scallops. 571: Mussel. 572: Slit shell.
573: Barnacles. 576, 577: Limpets. 578: Unidentified univalve in cross-section.

579: Pyrula. 580, 605: Barnacles. 581: Conch. 582: Cone shell. 583, 588: Triton
shells. 584: Giant clam. 585: Encrusting tunicate. 586, 597: Fistulana. 587: [*Villorit
cyprinoides*]. 589, 596, 601, 609: Unidentified univalves. 590: Lucine. 591: Cockle.
592: Jewel box. 593: Watering pot (bottom view). 594, 599, 607: Unidentified univalves
in cross-section. 595: Tellin. 598: Columbella. 600: Lingula. 602: Spindle shell.
603: Tunicate. 604, 608: Oysters. 608: Mussel. 610: Limpet (ventral view, showing
operculum). 611: Mesodesma.

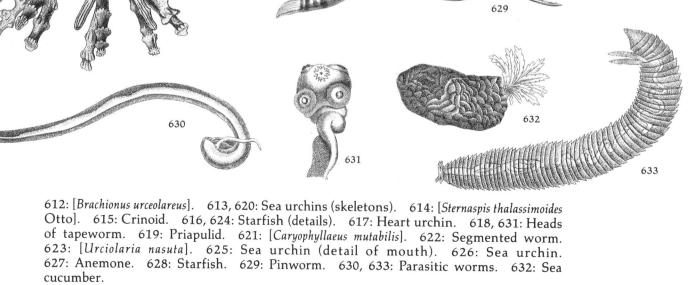

612: [*Brachionus urceolareus*]. 613, 620: Sea urchins (skeletons). 614: [*Sternaspis thalassimoides* Otto]. 615: Crinoid. 616, 624: Starfish (details). 617: Heart urchin. 618, 631: Heads of tapeworm. 619: Priapulid. 621: [*Caryophyllaeus mutabilis*]. 622: Segmented worm. 623: [*Urciolaria nasuta*]. 625: Sea urchin (detail of mouth). 626: Sea urchin. 627: Anemone. 628: Starfish. 629: Pinworm. 630, 633: Parasitic worms. 632: Sea cucumber.

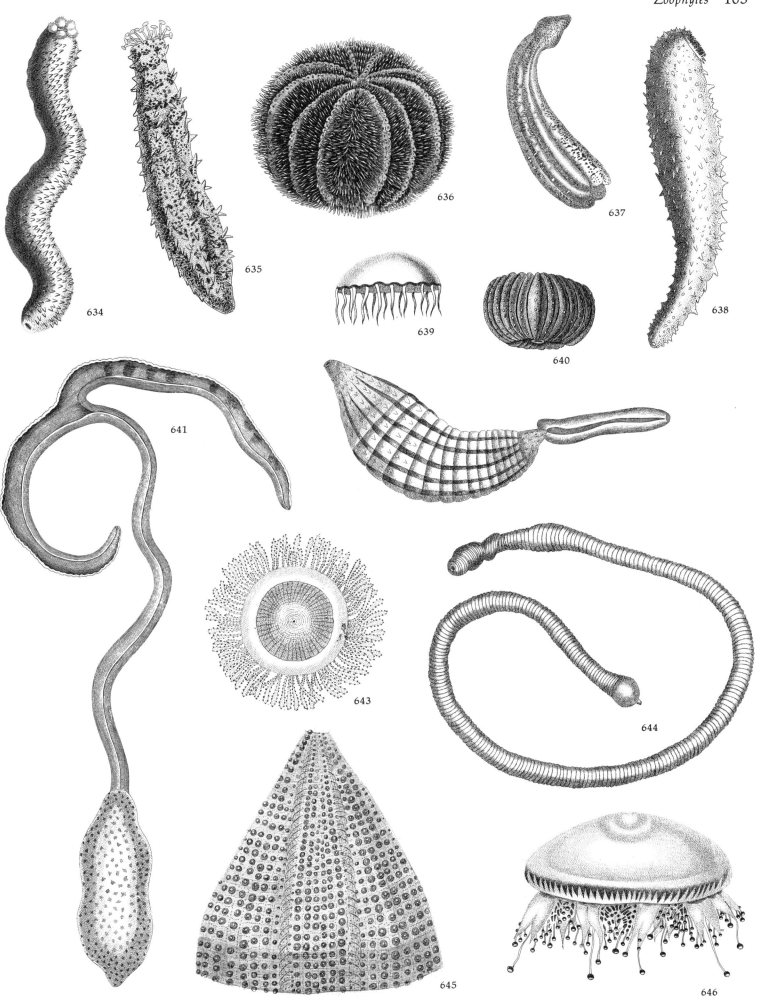

634, 635, 638, 642: Sea cucumbers. 636: Sea urchin. 637, 641, 644: Marine worms. 639, 646: Jellyfish. 640: [*Minyas cyanea*]. 643: Porpita. 645: Sea urchin (detail).

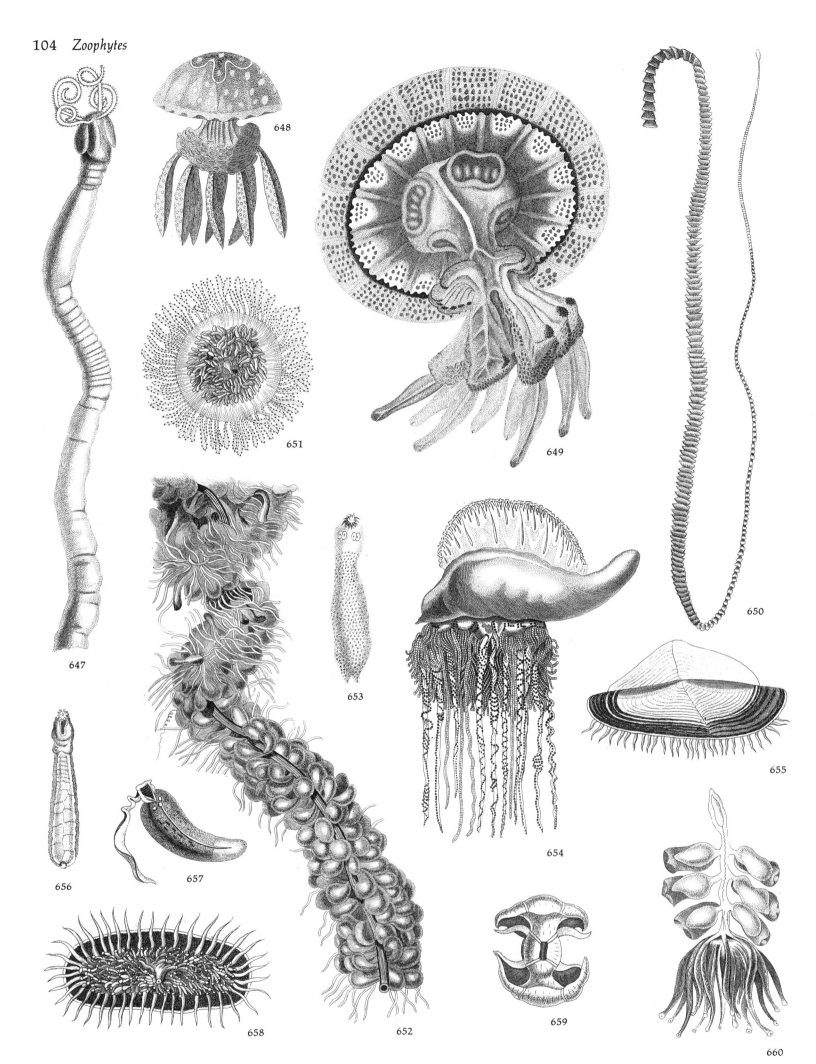

647, 653: Worms. 648, 649, 652, 660: Jellyfish. 650, 656: Tapeworms.
651: Porpita. 654: Portuguese man of war. 655, 658: Velella. 657: Marine
worm. 659: [*Alcinoe vermiculata*].

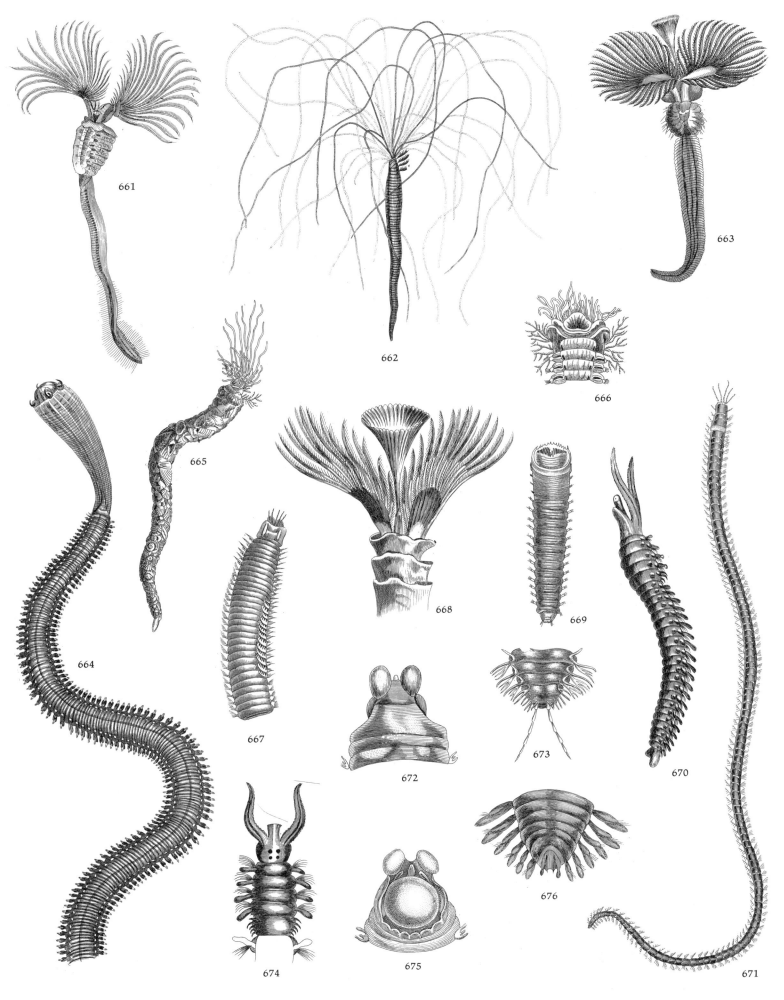

661, 663–665, 669–671: Worms.   662: Hydra.   666–668: Worms (details of heads).
672–676: Worms (details).

677–689: Crabs.

690

691

692

693

694

695

696

697

698

700

701

699

702-704, 706, 712, 713: Crabs.   705: Slipper lobster.   707: Shrimp.   708: Crab
(larval stage).   709: Cypris.   710: Water flea.   711: Crayfish.   714: Crustacean.

715, 717, 718, 727: Crabs.   716: Opossum shrimp.   719: Shrimp.   720, 721, 723–726,
728, 729: Crustaceans.   722: Shrimp.

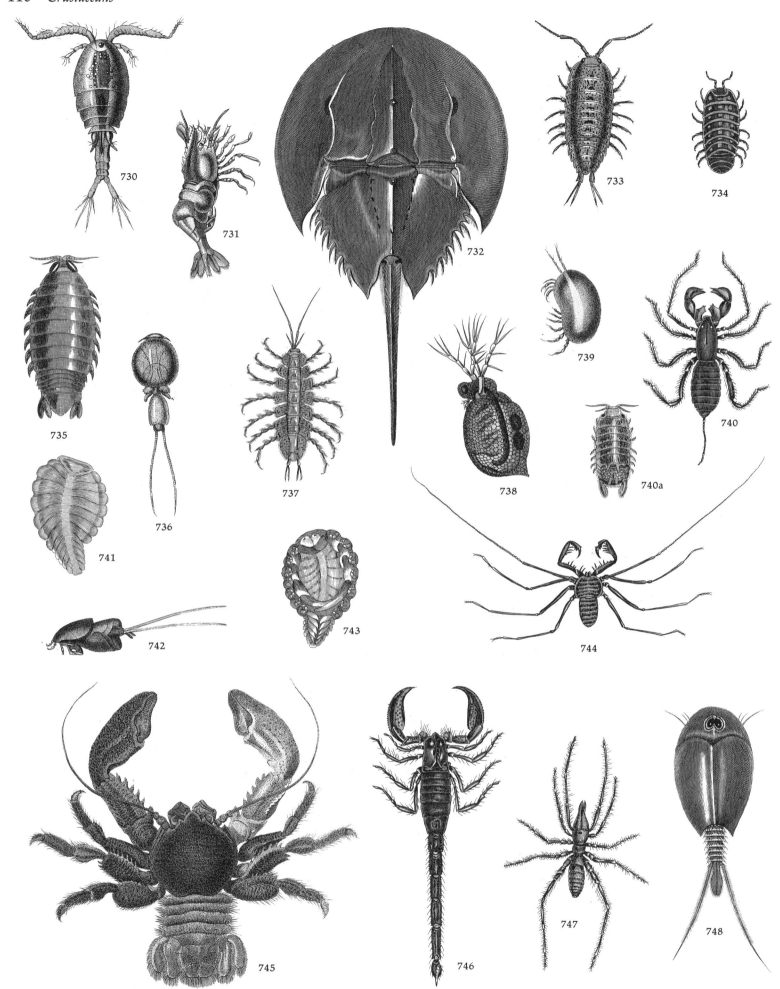

730: Cyclops.   731, 733–737, 740a, 741, 743, 748: Crustaceans.   732: Horseshoe crab.   738: Daphnia.   739, 742: Water fleas.   740, 746: Scorpions.   744, 747: Arachnids.   745: Porcelain crab.

763–768, 771, 775, 777–779: Spiders.   769, 772: Mites.   770, 774, 781: Arachnids.
773, 776, 780: Ticks.

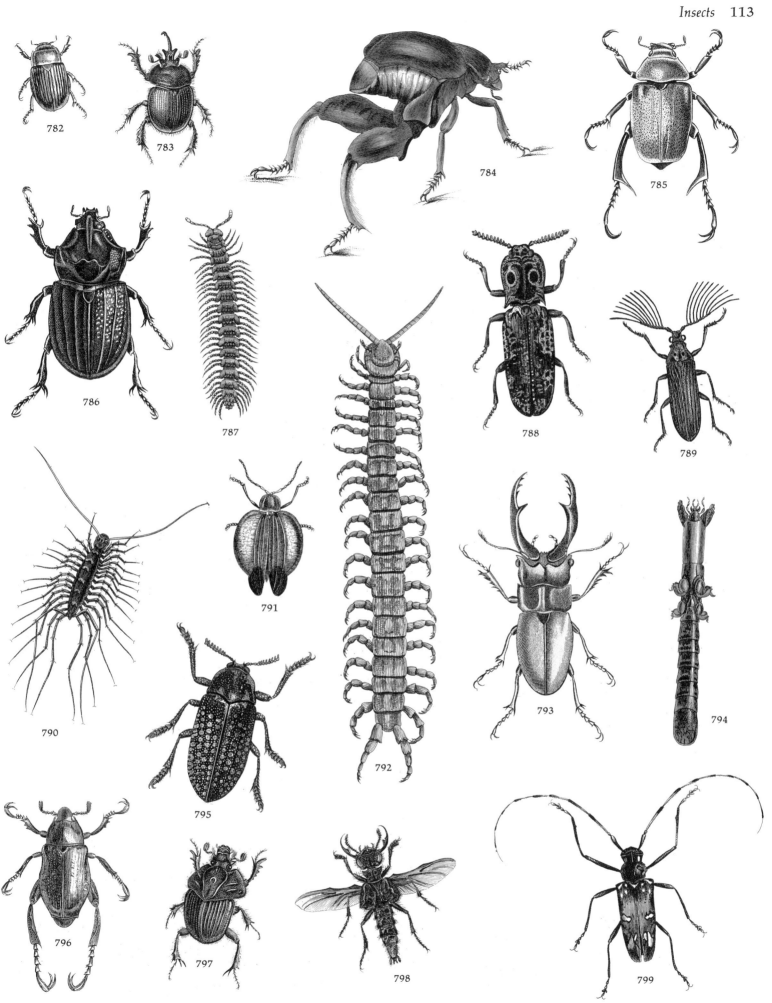

782, 785, 786, 788, 789, 791, 795–797, 799: Beetles.   783: Weevil.   784: Scarab
beetle.   787, 790, 792: Centipedes.   793: Stag beetle.   794, 798: Unidentified.

800, 803: Grasshoppers.   801: Weevil.   802, 804, 805, 810: Beetles.   806–809, 811: Bugs.   812: Cricket.

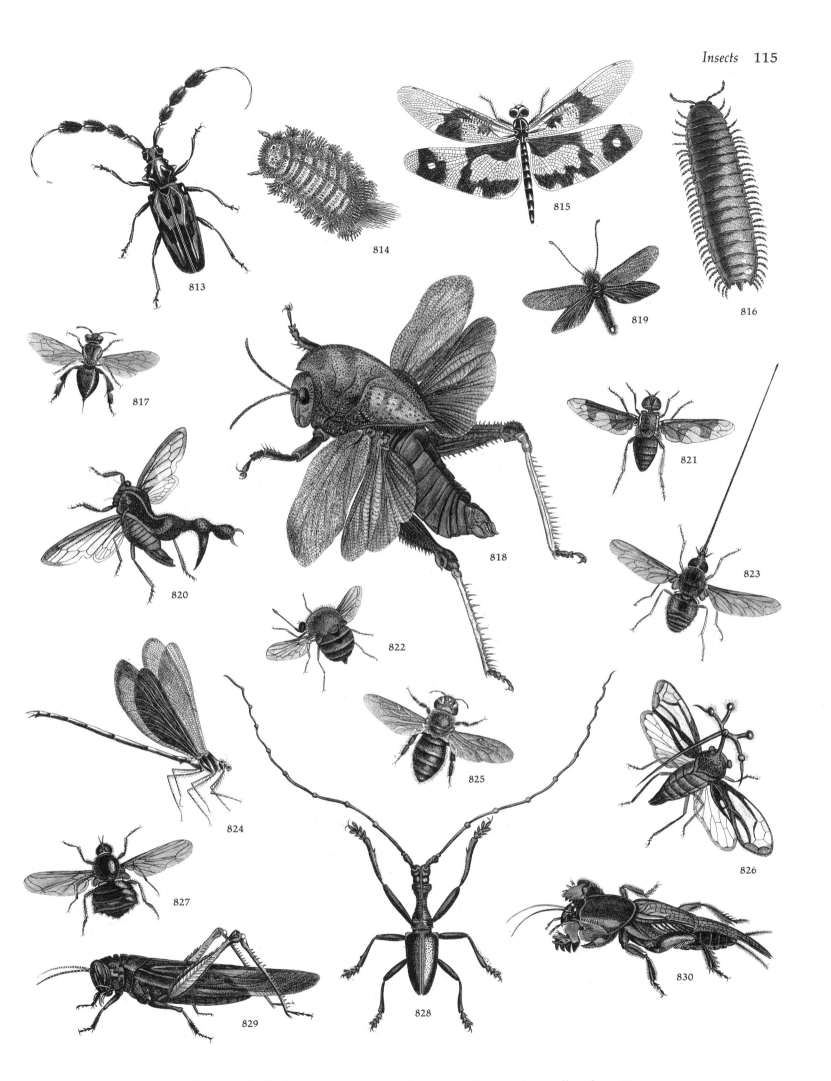

813: Bug.   814: Scale insect.   815, 819: Dragonflies.   816: Millipede.   817,
825: Bees.   818: Cricket.   820, 826: Cicadas.   821–823, 827: Flies.   824: Damselfly.
828: Beetle.   829: Grasshopper.   830: Mole cricket.

831–847: Butterflies.

848

849

850

851

852

853

854

855

856

857

858

859

860

861

862

863

864

865

866

867

848–851, 853–855, 857, 860–863: Moths.   852: Caterpillar.   856, 858, 859, 864–867: Butterflies.

Index

References are to figure numbers.